Child of
SORROW

A Novella by

GLORIA WEINBERG

PROLOGUE

This is a fictional account of a true story. The names have been changed to protect the privacy of those involved.

It is dedicated to every woman forced to surrender a baby for adoption, whether by society's mores or for reasons of her own conscience.

Many suffer from a unique type of post-traumatic stress, depression or other kinds of personality disorders, some of which manifest late in life.

But few ever completely recover from the experience. And no one ever forgets it.

CHAPTER ONE

From the back seat, I could see the muscle in my father's jaw bulge as he clenched his teeth.

"Go on," he said, without looking back. "Go knock on the door and see if this is the place."

The old two-story house sagged at the corners so that it seemed to frown at visitors. Paint that once was white had long ago turned gray and peeled away from the wood, as if, like me, it longed not to be there.

A slow freight train clacked along tracks no more than 100 feet from the back of the Safe Haven Home for Unwed Mothers. A couple of blocks away, the Dandee Bread Company spewed the overpowering scent of baking bread from stacks that rose above the factory, and I felt the now-familiar nausea rise in my throat with any odor – whether good or bad.

I knew this was it, even though there was no sign. I could see the silhouettes of pregnant females through the foggy windows upstairs. Pulling my topper close over my swollen belly, I stepped out of the car into an uncommon chill for a September night in North Florida.

Before I had climbed the steps, a short, sturdy woman in black-laced shoes and stockings opened the front door and gave me an artificial smile.

"You must be Vicki," she said, reaching up to tuck a strand of iron-gray hair back into the bun at her nape. "Are those your parents in the car? Why don't you go tell them to come on in, and we can get everything settled."

"They'd rather not," I said, staring at the housemother's stubby, overrun heels. "Daddy said I got myself in this fix and I can get myself out of it."

The smile on Mrs. White's face disappeared along with the Southern accent she affected, and she announced in clipped tones that it wasn't a matter of choice.

"You said on the phone that you're only 17, so there are papers your parents will have to sign, along with payment to be made."

I looked back over my shoulder at my parents. My father still clutched the steering wheel with the car engine running, while my mother stared at her hands in her lap.

I was afraid that Daddy might just drive away and leave me there.

I had never been 300 miles from home alone, and my voice trembled as I ran back and spoke to my father through the open side vent in the car window.

"The lady says you have to come sign some papers, Daddy."

A minute passed – it seemed like an hour – before he cut the engine and stepped out. He cupped his hands around a cigarette lighter and lit a Lucky Strike.

My mother stayed where she was.

"Aren't you going to come in, Mama?"

"You damn right she is," my father answered.

I searched my mother's face as she walked around the back of the car and into the light of a street lamp. She didn't look at me, and her expression was blank – drained of all emotion except humiliation.

Mrs. White pasted on another smile and extended her hand toward a small office on what must once have been the front porch.

"You're Frank and Rena Bayle, I take it?" she said, motioning for us to sit.

Daddy just nodded his head.

"Now, we will make Vicki's stay here as comfortable as possible, but you should know that all our girls are expected to follow strict rules of diet and conduct, and all are expected to do chores about the place.

"The residents are not allowed to receive packages containing any kinds of foodstuff, and we don't allow smoking.

"Two infractions will result in her being discharged from the home."

As she spoke, she pulled an ashtray from a desk drawer and held it out so that my father could extinguish his cigarette.

"Thank you," Mrs. White said, the practiced smile reappearing.

"In addition, the girls walk to the free clinic in groups of two or three as often as required. It's a two-mile walk, one way, but walking is good for girls in their condition, you know. It helps to keep their weight down and improves their general health.

"Now, how do you intend to pay? You can write a check for the full amount of $1,000, or you can break that up into monthly payments of $250."

My father's face darkened.

"I thought this place was run by some charity outfit. We don't have that kind of money, miss, so you're going to have to come up with something less than that or we'll have to go somewhere else."

"It's *Mrs.* White, sir, and I'm sure we can 'come up' with something that will work for you. Our fees are based on ability to pay, but you'll have to document that, you know, with income tax reports or something."

"Bullshit," Daddy said, standing up and taking Mama by the arm. "I ain't showing you nothing."

Mrs. White tapped a pencil on her desk and remained seated.

"Well, there is the Catholic Charities Home, but I think Vicki mentioned that you had some, um, religious objection to that? There is also the county home for girls that's free, but she'd have to be a resident of Duval County to go there. Perhaps there is a county home for unwed mothers where you live? Of course, then everyone will know that your daughter got herself pregnant."

Daddy stopped at the door, but stared straight ahead. Mama sat back down.

"I can give you $200 now; that's all we had in savings. I may be able to sell my hunting buggy and some guns or something to get more, but I don't know when or how much."

"I'll pay you back, Daddy, when I get back home. I'll get a job and work real hard and pay you back every penny."

Daddy looked down at Mama and the muscle in his jaw began to twitch again. "I guess I could sell my bird dogs," he said. "They're field trial champions, so they'd probably bring a good price."

"Oh no, Daddy, no! You can't sell Pal and Jack. You worked so hard to train them."

"Maybe you should have thought about that before you started screwing a football player," he said, looking at me for the first time since we left Clewiston that morning.

His eyes were cold and hard, and I quickly looked down at his feet.

It occurred to me that he really needed new shoes. The steel-toed work shoes he wore were scorched and scarred by welding sparks, and stained with motor oil.

Funny the things you notice at a time like that.

My father took four fifty-dollar bills out of his pocket and handed them to Mama, then walked out the door and stood on the stoop, lighting another cigarette.

My mother held the money out toward Mrs. White, who took it with a smile, in exchange for a release-from-liability form she asked Mama to sign.

"I'm sure everything will work out just fine, Mrs. Bayle. You can write to Vicki anytime you like, and she can call you collect once a week. Just remember, no cookies or candy, OK?"

Mama twisted a tissue in her hands and looked at a picture of a woman in a military-type uniform that hung behind the housemother's desk.

I was wondering who that was when Mama's answer caught me by surprise.

"It would be best if she didn't call home," she said. "Our phone is on a party line, you see, and my niece is living with us now."

I was stunned.

Mama scanned the room, which was empty except for the three straight-backed chairs in front of Mrs. White's desk, some gray metal file cabinets lined up against one wall, and a green-shaded lamp.

"Do I get to see the room where she'll be staying?"

"Oh, I'm sorry, honey. We don't allow non-residents inside because that would be an invasion of the other residents' privacy. She'll be in isolation for the first week or so, until we get her checked out at the clinic, you know, to make sure she doesn't have any communicable diseases or anything."

Mama flinched at that.

"What about when her time comes?" Mama said. "Will you call us when she goes into labor so that I can try to get here?"

"Someone will notify you when the time comes," Mrs. White said. "That's usually after the baby is born, but she'll be alright. They're good people down at St. Vincent's."

Tears streamed down Mama's face as she looked at me.

"We'll try to come back at Christmas," she said, "if we can save enough money."

Then she turned and walked out the door.

I covered my face with m y hands and sobbed.

CHAPTER TWO

"You'll sleep here until after your first medical exam, and then you'll be assigned to one of the dorms with the other girls," Mrs. White said, tossing a pillow and bedding onto a cot in a corner of a small upstairs porch.

The two semi-private rooms down the hall, she explained, were for those within a month of delivery.

"Most of the girls do not use their real names while they're here. They usually pick the name of a movie star they like or something like that. So, what would you like to be called?"

"I like Grace Kelly," I said.

"Very well. We'll call you Grace from now on."

"Long as you don't call me late for supper," I said, trying to lighten the mood.

Mrs. White was not amused, and when I announced that I had to use the bathroom, the housemother seemed unduly annoyed.

She turned on her heel and told me to follow her down the long hall that bisected the upper floor.

I kept my eyes glued to Mrs. White's girdled backside, but I could hear a radio playing behind the door of one room we passed, and boisterous conversation from either side when we passed between the two dormitories.

"Here it is," Mrs. White said, stopping in front of the door at the end of the hall and knocking once before opening the door. "You must always knock, because all locks have been removed from doors on this floor after a nasty bit of business in one of the semi-private rooms.

She leaned close to Vicki and whispered conspiratorially, even though no one else was in sight.

"One of the girls slashed her wrists in that room over there not long ago, you know," she whispered. "She nearly bled to death before we could break the door down and get her to the hospital."

Of course, I didn't know that. How could I know such a thing?

"Anyway, remember, there are ten to twelve pregnant women here most of the time, so do your business and don't dawdle. A bath time will be assigned to you later, along with your chore schedule."

I had begun to cry again, despite trying not to, and I didn't move.

"Well, do you have to go or not? I have a TV show to watch."

"Yes, ma'am, and do you think I could get something to drink?"

Mrs. White rolled her eyes and sighed.

"There are some paper cups in there, and you can get some water from the tap. If you have to come back again during the night, you are not to interact with any of the other residents, do you understand? You're in quarantine right now. You'll meet them all soon enough.

"Now, my room is right at the end of the stairs and I can hear everything that goes on up here, so you just mind your manners and you won't get in trouble."

Back in my room, I made the bed with sheets that smelled like roach spray and a thin cotton blanket full of holes. The room was cold, and an icy breeze whistled through screens that were crudely boarded over, with clear sheets of plastic stapled to the inside.

I sat on the end of the cot and put on the new flannel pajamas Mama bought me that had a cord at the waist, which could be loosened as my belly grew. I took a clean pair of bobby-sox from the suitcase I got as a graduation present and pulled them on to warm my icy toes. After a minute or so, I took out another pair and pulled them on my hands.

It was already past 9 p.m., which was lights out time, so I couldn't read. I brought the only three books I owned with me, even though I'd read them all before: Dandelion Wine, by Ray Bradbury; Breakfast at Tiffany's, by Truman Capote; and East of Eden, by John Steinbeck. The books were presents from Ava Duncan, whose husband, Lawrence, owned the Dixie Crystal Theatre at home in Clewiston.

I worked at the theater from age 13. I got my work permit a year early, see, because Mama changed the date on my birth certificate so that I could start school the same year as my cousin, Penny. Then Penny failed the first grade, so I was a year ahead of her all through school, and everybody else in my class was a year older than I was.

They wouldn't let you do that today, but back then, everything depended on your I.Q., and I was a real smart kid in that regard. Pretty stupid in other ways, though, as it turned out.

Mrs. Duncan usually sold tickets at the theater, and she was…well, she was real heavy, but uncommonly vain about her lovely hands and Georgia peach complexion. I was always her pet, because I would stand and paint her nails or rub cream on her hands when there were no customers for tickets or popcorn.

Most of the kids who came to the picture show were afraid of Mrs. Duncan because she wouldn't put up with any of their nonsense. She'd have you expelled from the theater for doing anything rowdy, like throwing popcorn or necking in the back aisle. But she was always nice to me.

That first night at Safe Haven I tried to sleep, but the freight trains seemed to travel mostly after dark, so there was the constant clatter of their wheels on the tracks, and the engines sounded a warning as they approached the intersections. Every change of shift at the bread factory was heralded with a long steam whistle, as well.

The home was only a block or so from a fire station – which turned out to be a good thing, since we had to call for paramedics so often. But it also meant sirens coming and going day and night, along with all the other city traffic.

I'd never been anywhere as noisy as that place in my life. In Clewiston, we had the smelly old sugar mill, but it was a long way from our house, which Daddy built close to the Hendry General Hospital where Mama worked as a nurse's aide.

Now that I think about it, there must have been ambulances coming and going from the hospital, too, but I don't ever remember hearing sirens. Just one way a small town is different from a city like Jacksonville, I guess.

The cot was hard and uncomfortable, and I soon gave up trying to sleep. I wrapped the thin blanket around my shoulders and stood at the window, looking down through the cracks at the circle of light beneath the street lamp. At the corner, I could see cars pull up to a Sinclair station, and from the opposite direction, I heard young male voices talking real loud and laughing. I couldn't see them at first, but suddenly, there they were under the street lamp, three of them. One held a beer bottle by its neck and whistled, looking up toward the windows of the next room.

"Hey, baby, want some of this?" he said, holding the beer above his head and cupping his – you know – with his other hand. "Come on down, sweet thang. You already knocked up. What's it gonna hurt?"

The other two boys laughed and poked each other, and then they walked away toward the filling station.

It made me think of an incident from my childhood, when I had peed in my pants and kids on the bus taunted me with, "Everybody kno-ows, everybody kno-ows."

I threw myself back on the cot and started to cry again, pulling the pillow over my head to muffle my sobs and smother my shame.

It was still dark outside when I woke with a start to what sounded like a school bell ringing.

At first, I didn't remember where I was, and when I did, I began to tremble so violently that the legs of the cot clattered against the bare wood floor. My breath hung in the air in front of me, and down the hall I could hear bare feet shuffling around and female voices mumbling.

I pulled off my PJs and slipped into a pair of sweat pants and a baggy hooded shirt that said Clewiston High School on the front and Go Tigers on the back. I pulled the hood over my head, tucking my long blonde hair inside.

When I stuck my head out the door, I saw a line of girls of all ages, all in various stages of pregnancy, waiting to use the bathroom.

One of the older ones looked back and told me – in a nice way – to stay in my room. "Someone will bring you a breakfast tray," she said, smiling. "Eve is cooking this morning, so we might get some oatmeal that isn't burnt, for a change." My belly roiled in revulsion, and my bladder was about to explode.

I sat back down on the cot, but left the door open so I could see when the others left, then crept down the hall to the bathroom.

Just as I lifted my hand to knock, I heard retching from inside. I backed against the wall with my hand over my mouth and waited.

After a few minutes, I heard the toilet flush and water running, and then Elizabeth Taylor walked out, lavender eyes and all, but much younger and with a pixie haircut.

"What you staring at, for God's sake?" the girl said. "Ain't you ever heard a pregnant woman puke before?"

She leaned back as she waddled by, following her belly.

"Bet you have, honey. Bet you puke, yourself."

It was a prophecy that came true as soon as I closed the door behind me.

CHAPTER THREE

I graduated fifth in my class at Clewiston High School, mostly because I seldom did homework and the subjects didn't interest me.

Except for literature.

I am a writer. I have known this for as long as I can remember, but no one except K.C. Bentley, my high school English "lit" teacher – and, when I was younger, my father – took me seriously.

I was, after all, Miss Sugar of 1958. People usually treated me like a pretty face with a shapely figure and an empty head, and although part of me resented that, I used it to advantage.

I managed, despite my mediocre grades in math, to snag two small grants from area civic clubs that would help with college expenses – if I could talk my parents into letting me go.

The Woman's Club awarded its scholarship to the applicant whose essay on "Why Education is Important for Women" was deemed best. My winning essay for the Lion's Club College Grant was titled, "What Makes America Great."

I had applied to and been accepted for admittance to the University of Florida – if I passed my entrance exams. I was so sure of myself, I'd even gotten a tentative room assignment at Barrett Hall, where one of my classmates would be. I had such big plans.

I knew it would be a hardship for my parents to send me to college, but I was determined to go. I was an only child, and my father had always told me I could do anything I put my mind to. I had put my mind to this.

No one in my extended family – eight siblings on my mother's side and nine on my father's – had ever gone to college. I wanted desperately to be a real writer, and perhaps to teach, like my mentor, Mrs. Bentley.

And then, just after graduation, I missed my first period.

I had already ended an affair with my steady boyfriend, Dick Molino, who was my age but a year behind me in school.

Dick had quickly taken up with a perky freshman cheerleader who was, as he put it – in my face, and nasty – "an innocent little thing."

When I told him I was pregnant, Dick made it clear he had no intention of marrying me or missing his senior year of high school.

"How do I even know the kid is mine?" he said.

I slapped his face then and left him standing in the driveway of his new girlfriend's home, where I'd confronted him.

I was crushed. I didn't know what to do, so I did nothing.

Abortion was not an option in 1959, and I was idealistically opposed to it, anyway. I could not kill a living thing, which was a great disappointment to my father, a life-long hunter.

Somehow, I was able to conceal my condition from my mother until I was about four months pregnant. Once a month, I made small cuts on my arms and legs, smeared the blood on Kotex, and left them on top of the bathroom trash, wrapped in toilet paper.

I adopted the fashion of the day made popular by Jackie Kennedy – clam diggers and a smock-type blouse.

The loose-fitting blouse conveniently concealed the obvious, but it helped that my mother did not really want to see.

Then one day when I was over at my best friend Ann's house, her brother poked me in the belly and said, "Whatcha got goin' on there?"

He was a college sophomore, and one of the cool kids.

I walked away toward Ann's bedroom, and Peter and his buddies burst out laughing.

Decades later, when I think about it, I still blush.

I had sucked in my belly and tried to walk in a straight line, without swaying my hips.

Evidently, I failed.

I was humiliated.

Peter saw me a few days later at an alumni dance, and he heckled me again.

"So, I've gained a little weight," I said. "What's it to you?"

My mother confronted me a short time later.

"You're three or four months pregnant, aren't you?" Mama said.

It was useless to deny it then, so I sat down on my bed and cried.

"If you had come to me in the beginning, Vicki, we could have done something about it," Mama said. "I know a doctor in Okeechobee who might have…"

I looked at my mother in horror.

"You want me to kill my baby?"

"It's not a baby at first, Vicki. It's just a mass of tissue. Women have miscarriages all the time and they just flush it down the toilet. They certainly don't fish it out and put it in a coffin!"

I dropped my head and cupped my hands protectively around my belly.

"I know I can't keep him, Mama, but there's a home for unwed mothers in Jacksonville," I said. "I saw an ad for it in the newspaper. I could go there, and they'll put the baby up for adoption when he's born.

"He'll go to a good home, Mama, with people who really want a baby and can't have one."

"What makes you think it's a boy, Vicki?" Mama said, the anger now drained and replaced with a look of profound sorrow.

"I just know," I said. "I felt him move already, and I just know."

Mama spun around and walked to her bedroom, slamming the door behind her.

※

"Mama? Are you OK, Mama?"

She opened the door, dried her eyes with her palms, then replaced her glasses.

"I don't know how I'm going to tell your daddy about this," she said. "He thinks the sun rises and sets in you. This is just going to kill him."

"It's my fault, Mama," I said, squaring my shoulders. "I'll tell him." Mama bit her lip and stared at me.

"No, I'll do it, baby," she said. "Your father has a terrible temper, and I'd rather he take it out on me than on you."

I thought about the whipping I got when I was not quite nine, and I could feel myself blanch with fear.

"He won't hit you, will he, Mama?"

"No, of course not! He'll probably yell a lot and go out and get drunk is all."

"I'm so sorry, Mama, really I am."

"I know, baby," Mama said, gathering me in her arms. "I know you are. It'll be OK, now. We'll figure out something.

"Did you save the number for that home in Jacksonville?"

CHAPTER FOUR

"Girls, settle down, now," Mrs. White said to the residents of the place I would live for the next five months.

At least I'm not alone, I thought. At least I'm not the only one who got herself in trouble. At least, my baby is going to have a chance.

Around the living room, residents slumped together on a battered old sofa and in overstuffed chairs. The furnishings were either discards from the homes of the Benevolent Volunteers who ran the home, or were donated by other area charities.

I was still trying to learn the residents' names: Elizabeth, the first one I met in the bathroom, who was a year younger than I; Shirley, who was only 12 and brought her baby doll with her; Marilyn, a coarse bleached blonde I guessed was in her 20s; Eve, 33, a rape victim who had three children at home; and Natalie, an overweight girl my age, who rarely spoke to anyone. Eve said Natalie had tried sniffing glue and kerosene to make herself miscarry before she was placed in the home. After I'd been there about a week, I noticed the ugly red scars on Natalie's wrists, so I figured she was the one Mrs. White had been talking about that first night.

I found out later I was wrong. That had happened months earlier.

I had trouble trying to remember the names of the other residents, and I often forgot to answer when someone called me Grace. I'd just stand there with this blank expression, which somebody thought was funny, so then they started calling me Gracie, after Gracie Allen, the well-known comedienne.

"Hey, Gracie," said a new, dark-haired girl of about 20, as she plopped down on the arm of the chair I sat in. "I'm Rebecca of Sunnybrook Farm, but you can call me Becky."

I liked Becky instantly. She was always smiling and telling jokes, and her dark eyes twinkled with mischief. Unlike the other residents, Becky didn't sit around crying and looking miserable all the time, and she was always plotting ways to sneak food out of the kitchen.

I started to move over to share my chair, but Becky shook her head and slapped her thighs.

"I don't think so, bird legs," Becky said. "Not with these thunder thighs and satchel butt."

The residents of Safe Haven were on a strict 1,800-calorie diet that was about three-quarters of what the clinic doctors said we needed for proper nutrition during pregnancy. The heavier girls may have benefitted from the loss of body fat. But those who were slender, like me, had no reserves from which to draw.

My legs quickly lost their shapely contour, and as my belly and breasts got bigger, my face and arms appeared gaunt.

We were always hungry. Three or more of us sometimes shared a pilfered slice of bread, and a big dill pickle or a banana meant one bite each for six or more.

Stealing fruit was risky, though, because Mrs. White kept a careful count of all foodstuffs, especially fresh fruit. A slice of bread or a pickle might go unnoticed; a piece of fruit would not.

We also had to be careful that little miss Shirley Temple never found out, or she would go straight to Mrs. White and tattle on us like the child she was.

"We have a special treat tonight," Mrs. White announced. "Brother Van Dyke, pastor of the First Lutheran Church, is going to lead our prayer meeting, and I expect you all to be on your best behavior."

Becky leaned over and whispered in Vicki's ear, "Let's hope he brought some real bread and wine for communion," which earned her a stern look from the housemother.

Being on your best behavior, in Mrs. White's opinion, meant appearing downtrodden and remorseful and kowtowing to her every demand.

A spot missed while scrubbing floors or washing windows was considered a personal affront. Such offenses often were rewarded by having breakfast duty or KP for two weeks in a row, which was fine by me. Getting up at 4 a.m. and cooking for 12 people was a small price to pay for filching an extra mouthful of oatmeal with a little margarine slipped into it.

I had always refused to eat oatmeal at home, but now it seemed like food for the gods – even without milk and sugar.

My most dreaded chore was laundry, when two girls were assigned to wash all the linens and soiled clothes for the entire residence. Every Monday, rain or shine, no matter how cold, the three wringer-type washing machines churned from dawn until everything was clean. An old drafty shed hard by the railroad tracks provided a little protection from the wind. But hanging the wet sheets and towels on the lines to dry was torture. By the time we were done, our hands and faces were chapped and stiff with cold.

We prayed for sunshine every Monday, but it always seemed to be the darkest day of the week.

If it rained before the clothes were dry, we had to sleep that night on our thin mattresses with no linens. Only the downstairs had heat, so we'd often sleep two to a bed and pile all our clothes on top of us for warmth.

Mrs. White's other favored punishment for "willful behavior" was requiring residents to be silent for a day, and doubling the time if you forgot and spoke. Those who displeased the housemother were given the thinnest blankets, sheets with the most holes, smaller portions of food, or milk soured with vinegar.

"This is not the Biltmore, and you are not the queen," she was fond of saying to anyone who dared complain.

Becky once retorted, "Yeah, well neither are you, ol' lady."

She spent the next day scrubbing the upstairs and downstairs toilets with a toothbrush, but she quietly hummed "You Ain't Nothing But a Hound Dog" while she worked.

The Rev. Van Dyke was a fire-and-brimstone preacher, whose baritone sermons probably could be heard at the corner filling station.

He liked reading to us from the Book of John, Chapter 4, and he drew comparisons between us and the Samarian prostitute Jesus encountered at the well.

"Still, you are not separated from the love of God because of your transgressions," he said. "You are already forgiven by your heavenly father, who gave up his only son for you. "Now, you must follow His example."

I bowed my head and prayed for courage.

———◦◦◦———

By November, it was bitterly cold in Jacksonville, and I had to walk to the clinic every other Wednesday. Blood tests revealed that I was RH negative, and there was some concern about the health of my baby. They explained that if my RH "titer" began to rise, they might have to induce labor prematurely. This rarely ever happens with a first baby, though, the physician's assistant said. But she also put me on prenatal vitamins with iron because I was anemic.

I was tired all the time because, for whatever reason, Mrs. White rode me pretty hard. I guess it was because I refused to suck up to her like some of the other girls did, and when she gave me grief, I showed no emotion. I kept everything locked up tight as a drum, and I guess that sapped a lot of my energy.

I felt much better after I started taking the vitamins, though, and I even got a little color back in my cheeks. The pills also improved my appetite, however, and it didn't need improving.

Despite the biting wind that blew in from the river laden with stench from Jacksonville's paper mills, I looked forward to getting out of the house and walking. I always tried to pair up with Becky at the back of the line, because she would sneak into a drugstore and buy a candy bar with money she hid in her shoe. We devoured it as quickly as possible, and stopped chewing whenever one of the other girls looked back.

Becky also was not above giving the finger to people who stared and whispered to each other as our pregnant troop passed by, some with arms linked together, giggling like the teenagers most of us were.

But the most recent trip to the clinic was a bad one for Becky. She was about three weeks away from term, and the doctor told her she had genital warts.

"That son-of-a-bitch," she said, when she told me about it. "It wasn't enough that the bastard got me pregnant, he gave me a venereal disease."

I had no idea what genital warts were, but Becky, who had been a student nurse, explained it to me.

The guy who got her pregnant was one of her instructors, she said, and he was married.

Mrs. White immediately placed Becky in quarantine, which was ridiculous since genital warts are sexually transmitted. It was just another way of humiliating Becky.

———◆◆◆◆◆———

As Thanksgiving approached, I was more homesick than ever. My Aunt Linda sent me The Clewiston News each week, but seeing news and pictures of hometown events just made me feel more alone.

I got regular letters from my mother, and an occasional cheerful card from Ava Duncan, but nothing from my cousin, Penny, with whom I had shared my room for nearly a year.

To this day, she has not forgiven me my sins, as if they were committed against her. For years, I kept hoping she'd come around, but she never did. She told me once, years later, that she wished me well, but she never wanted to see me or talk to me again.

"It isn't that I hate you," she said. "I just don't feel anything for you, and I never did."

It was like ripping a bandage from a raw wound. I'll never understand it, but I've come to accept it.

The cover story my parents invented was that I had enrolled in a cosmetology school in Jacksonville, and I couldn't come home for visits because I had a job wrapping gifts at Sears on nights and weekends to help pay my way.

I doubted anyone would believe I'd been in beauty school when I came home with my stringy peroxided locks now a dingy brown at the roots. I didn't bother with pin curls at night anymore, and I just kept my shoulder-length hair pulled back in a ponytail most of the time.

One night, I stood looking at my image in the mirror while I dutifully rubbed my belly with "Mother's Friend," a smelly concoction of camphor and oils that my mother said would help keep me from getting stretch marks.

Suddenly, I put the bottle down, walked down the hall to Becky's room and knocked on the door.

"Come on in, bird-legs," Becky said. "I know it's you, 'cause I can smell that stinkin' potion you keep rubbing on yourself."

"Do you have any scissors?" I said.

"I've got my bandage scissors from nursing school is all. Why?"

"I want you to cut my hair."

Becky cackled like a hen.

"Me? Are you kidding? I don't know how to cut hair. I barely learned how to cut gauze."

"How hard can it be?" I said, holding out a magazine called Health and Beauty. "See, it tells you here step-by-step: 'How to Get That Audrey Hepburn Look.' You just hold the hair out from the scalp and cut it about the same length all over, and make it jagged around the edges."

By the time lights out came, my formerly golden locks were in a pile on the floor, and the image that stared back at me in the mirror looked more like Groucho Marx than a pixie. Becky and I both got the giggles.

"I think maybe we need to thin it out some around the face," I said, then fell on Becky's bed in an uncontrollable fit of laughter.

A week later, Becky went into labor during the night and I never saw her again.

CHAPTER FIVE

On Thanksgiving, Major Brett, head of the Jacksonville Benevolent Volunteers and a primary backer of Safe Haven, arranged for us to have a traditional dinner prepared by her own cook. It was complete with a huge turkey, stuffing, green beans, mashed potatoes with gravy and cranberry sauce. One of the other volunteers even brought pumpkin pies and whole milk.

The smell was heavenly.

Mrs. White was doling out small portions of the feast when Major Brett showed up with her daughter Mary, a tall, statuesque beauty, and they demanded that the entire banquet be placed on the table.

I never learned Major Brett's real first name. The Benevolent Volunteers wore navy jackets and skirts, and had military titles – like captain or sergeant or lieutenant. Mary Brett was a professional singer and actress, though, who regaled us throughout dinner with a running commentary of jokes and even a few Broadway numbers.

We were dazzled.

When it came time for dessert, Mary was upset because there was no whipped cream for the pie.

"There's a convenience store just around the corner," she said. "I'll be right back." Soon she was back with canned whipped cream and vanilla ice cream.

"Sorry, guys," she said with a broad grin. "This is all they had left." I almost cried.

It was the happiest night I'd ever spent at Safe Haven, and it was the first time I didn't go to bed hungry.

I dreamt that night that Dick showed up at the door and told me he had changed his mind.

"I want to take you home and marry you," he said. "You can find a job waiting tables or something, and I can work after school and weekends. We can get by, and our parents will probably help us after the baby comes, don't you think?"

I woke to a scream coming from the bathroom at the end of the hall.

It was Elizabeth. Her water broke, only it wasn't just the amniotic fluid they had told us about; there was a puddle of bright red blood at her feet and more running down her leg.

By the time I got there, Mrs. White had made her way up the stairs, and she grabbed a towel and shoved it between Elizabeth's legs.

"Deane!" she shouted. "Lie down and hold this between your legs." I never knew Elizabeth's real name until that moment.

"Vicki – I mean, Grace – go downstairs and call the fire department," Mrs. White said. "Tell them we need an ambulance, quick!"

It wasn't until after I dialed that I realized I didn't know the address of the home. All the letters I got were sent to a post office box.

"It's the Safe Haven Home for Unwed Mothers," I told the dispatcher, "and it's not far from the Dandee Bakery. The railroad runs right behind it and it's a big old white house…"

"It's OK, miss," the dispatcher said. "The paramedics know where it is. Just stay on the line with me and tell me what's happening. Help is on the way."

"I don't know what's happening, except that this girl is having a baby and she's bleeding a whole lot," I said. "She's upstairs and I'm downstairs, so I can't see anything."

By the time I heard the sirens out front, Mrs. White had come back downstairs and unlocked the front door.

"They're here," I said into the receiver.

"OK, honey. You can hang up now."

The two men wore blue overalls and rubber gloves, and they carried a stretcher upstairs as if they were in no particular hurry.

Just like it's something they do every day, I thought.

Within moments, they were carrying Elizabeth, strapped to the gurney, back down the stairs to the waiting ambulance.

The sound of the siren had faded away in the night before anyone said anything.

"Aren't you going to follow them to the hospital?" I asked Mrs. White.

"Of course not," she said. "I can't leave you all here unsupervised.

"Now, Grace, since you're doing bathrooms this week, you can go upstairs and clean up that mess. And don't use the good towels. Use the cleaning rags."

What I wanted to say – what Becky would have said – was, "How will I know the difference?"

It was five days later when Elizabeth came back to the home to clean out her room and pick up her belongings.

She was pale and thin, and the thick mascara and cherry-red lipstick she always wore was gone. I almost didn't recognize her, because she looked so small – younger in some ways, much older in others.

She said she had something called placenta previa, and that she and the baby nearly bled to death before she delivered.

"You doing OK, now?" Eve asked.

"They wouldn't let me see her," Elizabeth said. "They wouldn't even let me see my baby."

Elizabeth waited with her suitcase on the front steps until a taxicab came for her. When she got in, she didn't look back.

Two new girls came to the home in December. One who called herself June was 16 and had no idea who her baby's father was. She'd been turning tricks since she was 14, she said. That's when her stepfather started renting her out to his buddies. Her mother kicked her out of the house when she got pregnant, and she'd been living on the streets ever since.

A Jacksonville cop picked her up and gave her the choice of coming to Safe Haven or going to jail.

I couldn't imagine why anyone would pay to have sex with a girl like June, who had rotten teeth and a disposition to match. She was rude, crude, vulgar and profane.

Patricia was just the opposite: a college girl who was quiet, cultured, and a devout Catholic. Well, she had been devout until she met some seminary student named Joe who evidently was sowing all his wild oats before taking on the mantle of celibacy.

I looked up the word "celibacy" in the dictionary that Mrs. Duncan sent me at Halloween. She put some candy corn in the package, too, but Mrs. White confiscated it. We had to open all our mail in front of her to make sure it contained no contraband.

I read my dictionary like most of the girls read their movie star magazines. I still do, if I don't have anything else to read.

Patricia's parents told her the only way to get back in the good graces of the Church was to give up her baby for adoption.

"I'm the eldest of seven siblings, and my mother is pregnant again, too," she said. "She just couldn't bear the shame of having a baby and a grandchild to raise at the same time."

"Holy shit!" June said, plopping down across the room. "You'd think she would want you to stay home and help with all those brats!"

"Oh, no," Patricia said. "My parents want me to become a nun, like we planned. That's why I couldn't go to Catholic Charities. They don't want this mistake to keep me from my calling."

———

About a week after Elizabeth left, I got a package from Mama with snowmen and Santa Claus stickers all over it. She said in a note she was sending it early because she knew I needed it. And, she said that she didn't think that she and Daddy would be able to come for Christmas, because Daddy was doing odd jobs for the sugar company in addition to his full-time job with the Corps of Engineers.

Mama said she had also taken on extra hours as a practical nurse at the hospital, mostly night duty taking care of a severely burned woman named Charity.

I knew all that extra work was entirely my fault, and I cried while I opened the package. Inside were a cap, scarf and mittens that Mama had knitted out of multicolored wool. To this day, it's the best present I ever got, and I put it all on and wore it every day, except for meal times.

The next week, Shirley Temple's parents came and took her home. She was as big as a house by then, but they had decided they would let Shirley keep the baby and raise it as their own. Shirley was thrilled.

"Now I'll have a real baby to play with," she said.

"Lord help it," June said.

It was the Monday before Christmas when June "split," as she had been threatening to for weeks.

While she was supposed to be doing laundry in the shed out back, she kicked out one of the loose boards and shagged it across the railroad tracks to meet up with an old boyfriend.

She gave Natalie five dollars not to tell until she was long gone.

Mrs. White was livid.

Eve said June had agreed to a "private" adoption, which Mrs. White had arranged, and now she was left holding the bag.

"Is that legal?" I asked.

"It is if the mother agrees to it," she said.

I was astonished. I was also frightened.

"Why would she do that?"

"Because the adoptive parents are willing to pay her," Eve said. "It's all about money with that woman. Why do you think we're on such a strict diet? She operates on a budget. The less she spends on food, the more she has to put in her pocket."

"But I thought…but the volunteers…"

"They don't know. Major Brett doesn't have a clue, and who do you think she'd believe, the housemother or you? You'd do well to keep your mouth shut, unless you want ol' lady White to kick you out on the street."

CHAPTER SIX

On Christmas Day, Major Brett and a number of volunteers came and brought us a big ham dinner, with macaroni and cheese, sweet potato casserole, broccoli (which I had never tasted before, but ate with relish), a Waldorf salad (also my first), corn muffins, chocolate cake and pecan pie. This time, they also brought whipped cream.

After dinner, the major handed out little gifts to each of us: an orange, candy canes, warm sox, gloves, and a New Testament.

"I hope these little offerings will bring you some small comfort," Major Brett said. "I know it's not much, but it comes with love."

Patricia and I cried, but the other girls just smiled politely.

"I wonder what was under her Christmas tree, a Porsche?" said June, who had shown up back at the front door on Christmas Eve with a black eye and a missing front tooth.

Her reappearance brightened Mrs. White's Christmas enormously.

But sometime during the evening, someone "dropped a dime" on Mrs. White. I never learned for sure, but I'd bet it was Eve, who was due to deliver soon and figured she had nothing to lose. She still had not made up her mind whether she would keep the new baby or give it up for adoption.

"I guess it will depend on whether it's white like my other children or black, like, well you know," she said. "I just don't think anyone in my family could handle that."

At the time, I didn't think that made her a bad person in any way. After all it was 1959, and people in the South had completely different ideas about such things then.

It did make me start thinking about what my mother had said about abortion, though. Maybe it wasn't always wrong. Maybe, sometimes, say in rape cases like Eve, it could be the right thing to do.

I was getting ready for bed a few nights later when Major Brett knocked on my door. "The girls tell me that Mrs. White has persecuted you ever since you came here," she said.

"Well, that may be true," I said. "I can't say. I have no other place to go."

Major Brett stood in the doorway, tears streaming down her face, and made a promise.

"No other girl will have to go through what you've been through, Vicki," she said. "We didn't know. She has in effect, been selling babies. She has been dismissed, and we intend to prosecute. I am so sorry."

What could I say? Why? How could you let that happen? Where were you when I needed you?

"They call me Gracie, here," I said, and then I let her hug me, while my baby recoiled in my belly.

She backed away and waited, but I had nothing else to say.

Once you have lost the ability to trust, it's hard to get it back.

I trusted no one.

There's a part of me, half a century later that still has trouble trusting.

By mid-January, all the girls who were at the home when I first got there and the ones who came right after me were gone, except for Eve – and June, who tended to come and go as she pleased.

Our new housemother was a black woman named Mable McGill, who had been the fill-in housemother on Mrs. White's days off.

We all loved Mable, because for one thing, she preferred to do all the cooking herself, and for another, she treated us like human beings. She also asked us to call her by her first name.

The difference between Mrs. White and Mable was like night and day – no pun intended.

Mable was kind and compassionate, and she was a wonderful cook. She made collard greens and fried cornbread; grits and eggs with homemade biscuits; fried chicken with rice and tomato gravy; and at night, if we were hungry, we could just go in the kitchen and help ourselves to milk and cookies.

She even let us go with her in her beat-up old Volkswagen van to the Farmer's Market sometimes. There were only seven of us at the time, so we could squeeze in, even though we all had picked up weight rather quickly once Mable came. We got to pick out vegetables we'd been craving, like corn-on-the-cob, or yellow squash, or butter beans, and I think sometimes Mable paid for those things out of her own pocket.

It was like a different place.

When the twins came to Safe Haven, things got a little strange, but somehow, we managed to laugh about it. I guess we'd all grown a little jaded by then.

Cassie and Candy, 15-year-old identical twins, came in about three weeks apart and the same guy impregnated them both. I think he was a relative – an uncle or something – but that's just what I heard.

It was really weird. You'd talk to Cassie in the kitchen, then go upstairs and see Cassie coming out of the bathroom. Only it wasn't Cassie, it was Candy.

I could only tell the difference because Candy was farther along than Cassie, and tended to be a mouth breather.

I was just getting used to seeing the twins when this gray-haired woman named Katherine came in, about six months pregnant.

She said she was only 44, but I swear, she looked ten years older. My mother was only 37, for heaven's sake. I just couldn't get over that.

Evidently, her husband had run off with a younger woman when he found out Katherine was pregnant, and then, when she started to show, she lost her job as an executive secretary. She said she had no intention of raising a baby alone.

She was quite bitter, but who could blame her?

Every time we had "group counseling sessions," (which was, in fact, indoctrination by social workers about the wisdom of surrendering our babies for adoption), Katherine would take notes in shorthand.

It was pretty impressive to watch, because even when more than one person was talking at the same time, she never asked anyone to repeat anything.

"What the hell you doing?" June asked her once. "Writing a book or something?"

Katherine said, "No, I'm just practicing my stenography."

That's when I started thinking about writing this book.

I kept my notes in a journal in longhand, though. I never was that good at shorthand, even though I took a class in high school.

⸻❖⸻

On February 7, eleven days before my due date, I started having contractions. I thought it was just gas, because that night Mable had made a big pot of black-eyed peas with rice and pork chops and sliced tomatoes and sweet iced tea. I ate way too much, and I told myself I was just paying for it now.

I was going down the hall to talk to Eve when I felt my belly get hard as a rock, and when I doubled over in pain, there was this big gush of liquid down the leg of my pajamas. I couldn't believe how much it hurt.

Eve heard me yelling her name, and heads started peeking out doors up and down the hall.

Someone went down to tell Mable, and she came up and took me back to my room and told me to lie down while she called Mrs. Brett, and then the fire department.

When she came back, she said the dispatcher for the fire department told her there had been a real bad wreck on the highway, and for us to time the contractions and call them back when they were two minutes apart.

By midnight, the contractions were still coming three or four minutes apart, but they were lasting more than a minute.

I thought I would split in half.

Mable sat by my bed and held my hand while she hummed "What a Friend We Have In Jesus." I tried to be quiet, but soon, I couldn't hold back the screams, and Mable couldn't take it any longer.

She sent one of the twins downstairs to call Mrs. Brett again, who told her to call for a taxi.

"She want me to put this chile in a cab by herself to go the hospital?"

"I'm just telling you what the lady said, Mable," Cassie said, popping the bubble gum forever in her mouth. "So I done called one. They said it would be about 20 minutes."

I screamed for my mother, and Mable wiped my brow with a washcloth.

"We gone get you up now baby and get you downstairs so you'll be ready when the cab comes," she said. "You tell me when this pain starts to ease off, and we'll go right then."

Mable told Candy to grab a blanket and some towels to cover one of the chairs in the living room, and she took off the terry cloth robe she was wearing and put it around my shoulders.

I only made it to the first landing when the next contraction dropped me to my knees, and by the time I got to the chair, the cabbie had arrived and started blowing his horn.

"C'mon, move it," he said as Eve and Mable helped me into the back seat. "I ain't interested in delivering no babies tonight.

"I done it before. Ain't my thing, and it makes a mess in my cab."

The ride to St. Vincent's Hospital was a blur of sound and light, and then a blast of cold air as a doctor and two nurses met the cab at the emergency entrance with a stretcher. I remember watching the tiles in the ceiling with all those little holes in them as they rolled me down a long dark hall. I thought they looked kind of like a honeycomb.

Then people were gathered on each side of me, holding onto the sheet I was on and someone shouted, "Lift on three: one, two, three."

Just as I landed on the new bed in the maternity ward, I had another contraction – the worst one yet – and I screamed again.

"Cut that out this minute," a woman's voice said. "Breathe through your mouth, and don't bear down. I'm going to prep you now."

She shoved a bedpan underneath me and hung an enema bag on a pole beside the bed, and then she began to shave my pubic hair.

People were walking back and forth in the long room, where five or six other women were in labor, and there were no screens or anything at the ends of the beds. Curtains that were supposed to provide some privacy were all pulled back to the heads of the beds, so when she shoved that plastic thing up my butt and released the clamp on the bag of water, everyone could see and smell the outcome.

"Are you done?" she said, finally.

"I don't know. I think so. Can't you pull that curtain around?"

"This ain't no private room, girlie, and I have to check on everybody in here."

After she cleaned me up a bit, a doctor came in, pulled a glove on his hand and shoved it inside me.

He put his other hand on my belly and pushed down, just as I started having another contraction.

"This your first baby?" he said, like he was asking about the weather. "Now, the next time you have a contraction, I want you to start bearing down, understand? You bear down as hard as you can, just like when you're having a bowel movement."

Then he stood up, stripped off the glove and threw it in the trash, and pulled the curtain all the way around the end of my bed.

Now? I thought. Now, you're going to give me some privacy?

<hr />

I could hear him talking to the nurse at the end of the bed. She came in a few minutes later and started an IV drip in a vein in my left hand. She didn't even turn on the overhead light, but just propped her small flashlight on a towel that was on the bedside table and worked by its feeble illumination. She stuck me three or four times before she found a vein that didn't collapse – which she blamed on me for being dehydrated – and then she started a saline drip.

"We're going to give you a little Pitocin now to help speed this up a bit, and doctor has ordered something for pain if you need it."

"I need it," I said, as politely as I could with my teeth clenched.

She looked at me like I was something she had wiped off her shoe, but then she left and brought back a shot of something she injected into the port of the IV.

Two things happened almost immediately: my contractions got closer together, and I didn't care.

I think I dosed off for a couple of minutes, because I remember a dream about bees crawling out of the holes in the ceiling, and then they were all stinging me at once between my legs.

I started screaming for help when I looked down and saw it was not bees between my legs but my baby's head.

"You have got to stop this yelling," the nurse said as she jerked back the curtain, and then she let out a pretty good yelp herself.

"Call the doctor and help me reel this one into the delivery room," she said to someone I couldn't see.

The next thing I saw were the football lights. They were all around me in this green room where everybody wore green masks and green overcoats. Then someone put a clear mask over my face and told me to take a deep breath, and I heard a little mew – like a kitten, almost. Then someone said, "It's a boy: a big, beautiful boy."

Then the bees came back, and that's the last thing I remember until I woke up the next morning, back in the maternity ward.

CHAPTER SEVEN

I tried to sit up in the bed when the aides started bringing in the breakfast trays.

I was absolutely famished. I was feeling pretty good, actually, until I went to swing my legs over the side of the bed. Next thing I knew, there was a nurse on one side of me and an orderly on the other, and I wondered which one of them had stabbed me.

I found out later that since I had delivered my baby without the aid of an episiotomy (that's where they cut you to make delivery easier) I had a vaginal tear that went nearly to my rectum and required about 10 stitches to close.

I guess that was what felt like bees stinging me that last time; that was when they were sewing me up. I thought it felt like someone had pushed a billy goat up my rear end, and that made me smile, because I remembered Daddy saying that after he had surgery for his hemorrhoids.

The nurse pushed me back on the bed and told the orderly to raise the head of the bed with the little crank at the end of the bed. She showed me the control button I could use to raise and lower the bed for myself and another button I could use to call a nurse, if I needed one.

"We are very busy on this floor, so don't call unless you really need help."

The orderly pushed my bed table across in front of me and lifted the little silver cover from my breakfast tray. It held a bowl of Cream of Wheat, two pieces of toast, coffee and milk. But there were two patties of real butter and four packets of sugar and a tiny cup of cream for the coffee.

I devoured it all, and asked the orderly picking up trays if I might have more.

I can give you a banana, little lady, but that's all the more I got," he said.

"That would be wonderful," I said. "Thank you so much."

About an hour later, nurses started to bring the newborns to their mothers.

As soon as I heard the first one cry, the front of my gown got wet.

"Where's my baby?" I asked a nurse, who passed me by as if I were invisible. "Aren't you going to bring me my baby?"

Nobody answered, until I began to scream.

"I want my baby!"

"Shut up!" a nurse told me. "You're not supposed to see your baby, because you signed away your rights to him."

"I didn't sign anything!" I said. "Bring me my baby!"

The other mothers stared at me, somewhat furtively, while they fed their babies. Like maybe I would run up and take the child they cuddled. Like I wanted anyone else's baby but my own.

Another nurse came in then and gave me a shot. I don't know what it was, but it knocked me out cold.

Later that morning, a social worker I remembered came into the ward and stood by my bed.

"They tell me you've been causing a disturbance here," she said.

"I'm sorry," I said. "I only want to see my baby. Can you help me?"

"That will just make it harder on you, Vicki," she said. "It's better, by far, if you just put this incident behind you and get on with your life."

Across the room, a baby cried, and as soon as I heard, milk ran down to my belly.

"Please," I said. "Please just let me see him. Just let me hold him one time. I won't ask for more."

It was a lie, of course.

As soon as they laid my baby in my arms, he turned his head, searching for my breast with his little rosebud mouth, and I kissed it, before I pulled down one side of my gown.

It was the sweetest kiss I ever had.

While he nursed, I opened the swaddling clothes and counted all his fingers and toes and stroked his downy head. He curled his little fist around my finger, like he was holding on to life.

And I was certain – beyond a doubt – that I could never give him up.

I was wrong, of course.

The only thing I knew for certain was that they would never let me keep him.

That night, they let me call my mother on a pay phone in the hall.

She didn't know.

"You had it?" she said. "But you weren't even due yet. They said they were going to call, when you…"

"It's a boy, Mama, and he's the cutest little thing you ever saw. You'd love him if you saw him, Mama. I know you would."

"You saw it? You weren't supposed to do that, Vicki. We talked about this, remember?"

"I had to, Mama. I just had to, and I don't want to give him up. Please, Mama. Please let me bring him home."

I heard a click, and then my mother said someone else had picked up the phone.

"This is a party line, Vicki. Have you forgotten that?"

"I'm sorry, Mama, but I can't help it. He's my baby, and I want to keep him."

"You cannot do this to us, Victoria. After all you've put us through? For once in your life, you have to think about someone other than yourself!"

Then the line went dead.

I hung the receiver back on its hook, and the nurse wheeled me back to my room.

I didn't shed a tear. I think a part of me died then. I was too numb even to cry.

———✦———

The third day I was in the hospital, I started running a fever. A very high fever.

They did a lot of blood tests and other stuff, and they told me I had a kidney infection.

The nurse said they couldn't discharge me until my fever went down.

I didn't care, as long as they kept bringing me my baby every four hours.

I had to feed him from a bottle by then, of course, because they were giving me medication to dry up my milk. Still, I lived for those moments. While the other mothers moaned and groaned when the nurses came in with the babies during the night, I was always wide awake and eager to see my son. I named him Brian Keith.

On the sixth morning, the nurse didn't bring him with the other babies.

"Where's my baby?" I asked.

She didn't answer, but then a different nurse came in and gave me another one of those knock-out shots.

"Your baby is gone," she said. "The adoption agency came and took him."

It's the last thing I remember before I passed out.

And I never saw my baby boy again.

———

The social workers came to my room the next day with papers for me to sign, surrendering my baby for adoption. It was like trying to sign my name with a razor blade; it was like signing my own death certificate.

When they left, I stood at the window and watched an Asian girl weeding the begonias that were planted along the entrance to the hospital. A yellow cur sniffed at her heels, while two men in a black car stood waiting for the social workers to return.

They tried to call the dog to them, but he spooked and ran away.

As the two women they were waiting for emerged, one of the men got into the driver's seat and the other opened the back door for the social workers.

Salty-haired men and sugar-toned women, I thought, clothed in contempt.

I didn't cry until they started laughing.

Then I beat on the window and screamed, "I want my baby back! He's mine. I know his name."

One of the women looked back at me as the black car pulled away.

But nothing really mattered after that. Not the red begonias or the yellow dog, and surely not the lilies that bloom for just a day and then are gone – like my precious baby.

But oh, how beautiful they are, I thought. *How lovely and how sweet.*

EPILOGUE

Within two years of returning home, I graduated from a West Palm Beach beauty school, married a nice, responsible older man, and had a baby girl. A year later, we had a son, and three years after that, another daughter.

After 18 years, we divorced and I got a job at the local newspaper. I started out as a news clerk and worked my way up to reporter, photographer and finally, several different editors' positions.

How I did this with no formal education beyond high school still surprises some people.

I volunteered.

If there was a trial or a city council meeting or a wreck that needed coverage and there was no one else to go, I said, "Send me."

And, I studied the work of every journalist I knew to determine what sets the best of them apart from the hacks. I learned how to be better by doing better.

After seven years of being single, I married the man who has turned out to be the love of my life.

He loves and respects my now-grown children, and we both have a friendly relationship with my ex-husband, who also remarried.

In 2001, I retired from the newspaper and began writing my first novel.

It was easily the happiest time of my life. I started painting again, a passion I had abandoned when I went to work, and I wrote at my leisure, without the pressure of deadlines or competition.

And then I got the call that changed my life forever.

For years, off and on, I had been searching for my first-born son. To find him was all I needed, I thought, to make my life complete.

As it turned out, he had been looking for me as well. And I knew somehow, as soon as the Jacksonville number appeared on my Caller ID, that my long wait was over.

The caller identified herself as an adoptions volunteer with Catholic Charities, which took over the moldy, water-damaged files that were left behind when the unwed mother's home I was in closed its doors decades before.

"It's a wonder we were able to find anything," she explained. "The files were just stacked in a room in cardboard boxes."

Molly asked me a series of questions to ensure she was speaking to the right woman. I could barely contain my excitement as I answered. But there was something in the tone of her voice that frightened me: an absence of joy. And then, she gently said the words that shattered my soul.

"I'm sorry to tell you that your son is now deceased," she said. "But I have a letter from his widow that she would like me to forward to you. Is that OK with you?"

I couldn't speak. A scream rose in my throat, but it died there, with my hope. Finally, I was able to give my address so she could send the letter.

"How did he die, and when?" I managed to ask.

Molly said my son had died — just a few weeks before we would, no doubt, have found each other — of an accidental overdose of Oxycontin, the notorious pain medication so much in the news these days.

Like me, he had suffered from degenerative disc disease, and he had had several back surgeries. When his doctors sought to wean him from his usual pain medications, my Webmaster son went online and obtained the drug he'd heard was a "miracle drug" for pain, but one he'd never taken.

He also suffered from sleep apnea. He had shoveled snow from the driveway of his Pennsylvania home that day, then watched sports and drank a few beers with some buddies. When they left, he took the pill and fell asleep without his apnea mask. He died of respiratory arrest brought on by the combination of drugs and alcohol.

I was torn between grief and rage.

"Why would God allow you to find me now, if he was never going to allow me to hold my son and tell him how much I loved him?" I asked. "All those years, all those prayers were for nothing?"

Molly answered my questions with a question.

"Do you have grandchildren?" she asked.

At the time, I did not.

"You do now," she said. "Two little girls, ages 4 and 5."

I learned later that I have a lovely daughter-in-law with an indomitable spirit and an infectious laugh. She had recently moved with my granddaughters, into a new home outside of Jacksonville, where my son grew up.

My son had been estranged from his adoptive parents for years, his widow said.

And she told me another cruel fact; the family they claimed would be better than any I could provide as a 17-year-old with no husband and no way to support a child was far less than ideal.

"His adoptive parents were so abusive that he left home at 15 and went to live with his best friend," she said.

It was a dagger through my heart.

I later learned I also had a 21-year-old grandson, by my son's first wife, and that he had a 2-year-old daughter and a newborn son.

Imagine that. Me, a great-grandmother.

Now, I am blessed with seven grandchildren, and I consider each one a unique gift from God.

My first visit with my son's widow and his girls brought hugs and tears, joy and pain. She brought along a family album of photographs of my late son as a baby, as a child grinning from behind successive birthday cakes, as a proud young man in an Air Force uniform.

I stroke his baby pictures, kiss them like I once kissed his downy head, and I weep.

I now have videos of my son playing with his children in the snow, singing karaoke, sharing holiday meals with his in-laws. I hear his voice as he videotapes the birth of his daughter, builds a deck onto his home, hides Easter eggs for my granddaughters.

And I smile through tears.

While he lived, my son knew the joy of his "children's faces looking up, holding wonder like a cup."[1]

And when he died, by the grace of God, my son was loved. I draw comfort from that.

———⊰⊹⊱———

---

[1] From "Barter," a poem by Sara Teasdale

ABOUT THE AUTHOR

Gloria Taylor Weinberg is a fourth-generation Floridian who retired from the Fort Pierce Tribune after 22 years as a journalist. She received numerous awards from the Florida Press Association and the Florida Society of Newspaper Editors for her columns, features and explanatory reports, including the 2000 Gold Medal for Public Service.

Weinberg also paints, with a special love for capturing the flora, fauna and unique light of her native state on canvas. She lives with her husband, Mark, and Dudley, their spoiled cocker spaniel, in Fort Pierce, Florida.

Her debut novel, *A Homicide in Hooker's Point*, earned a 2011 Royal Palm Literary Award from the Florida Writers Association.